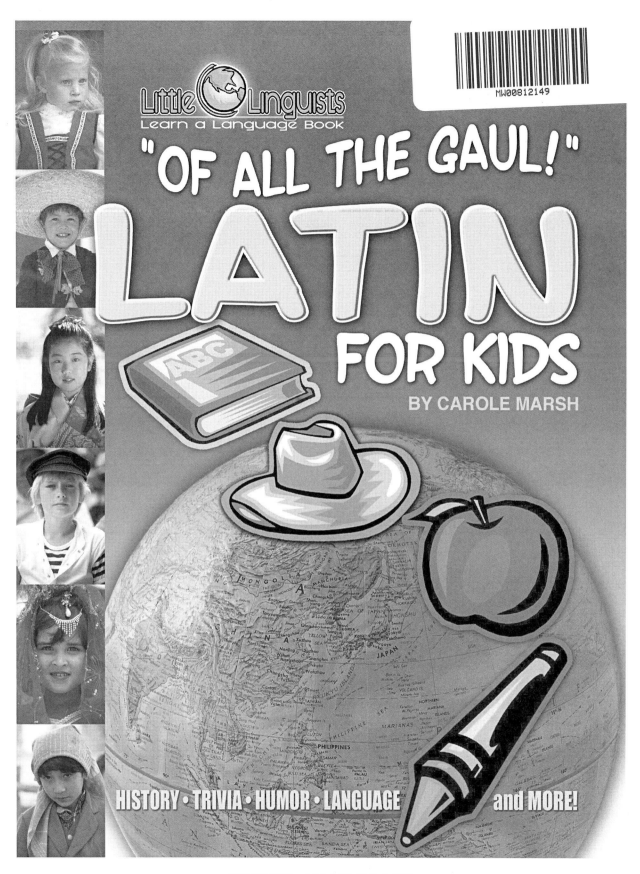

Little Linguists
Learn a Language Book

"OF ALL THE GAUL!"
LATIN
FOR KIDS
BY CAROLE MARSH

HISTORY • TRIVIA • HUMOR • LANGUAGE and MORE!

EDITOR: CHAD BEARD
COVER DESIGN: VICTORIA DEJOY
GRAPHIC DESIGN & LAYOUT: CECIL ANDERSON AND LYNETTE ROWE

Published by

GALLOPADE™
INTERNATIONAL

800-536-2GET
www.gallopade.com

Gallopade is proud to be a member of these educational organizations and associations:

The National School Supply and Equipment Association (NSSEA)
National Association for Gifted Children (NAGC)
American Booksellers Association (ABA)
Association of Partners for Public Lands (APPL)
Museum Store Association (MSA)
Publishers Marketing Association (PMA)
International Reading Association (IRA)

Carole Marsh Language Books

Math Books

Reading and Writing in the Real World!

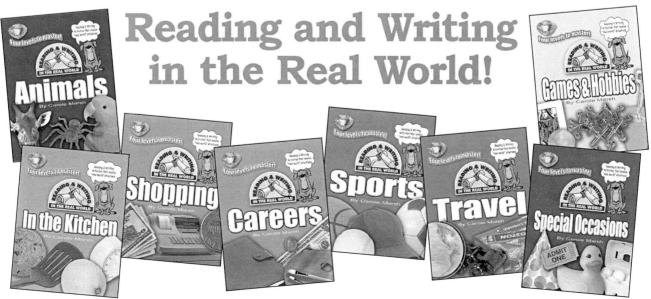

Word From the Author

Did you know that Latin words are used in the English language every day? Everybody thinks that it might be hard to learn a language... but not if you *already* know it!

My son, Michael, and I decided to see if we could learn one language a week one summer.

That summer resulted in *four* books that teach languages to kids. It's easy when you're having fun. We made a game of finding out how many foreign words were used in English.

Sometimes, because a language sounds strange to us, we think that it is very difficult to learn. In our rapidly expanding society, it is becoming more and more important to be able to communicate, often in another language!

Imagine, also, how much nicer a trip to another country is when you can speak to the natives in their own tongue. Although Latin is not in use today (except in some churches), it is the basis of all the European Romance languages. Knowing Latin can help you learn other languages—including English!

I wanted to show how easy learning a language could be when I started this series. Kids find my language books fun and easy to understand. So, enjoy this book in the spirit in which it was written. Have fun!

Carole Marsh

NOTE: This book is an "introduction" to the language. The focus is on why the child should learn some of the language, what the language is, and that they may already know many words in this language. The goal of this book is to get a child excited about the language, familiar with a few of the more common words or phrases they will encounter even in English texts, and eager to take a next more traditional step in learning the language. For languages not in the "ABC" alphabet, the "Romanized" or transliterated version of the language is used.

WHAT IS LATIN, ANYWAY?

A language, of course—but a language strongly tied to the history and the culture of the Roman Empire.

At first, the Romans had two versions of their Latin language. They had an official version—"high class Latin" used for business, literature, and speeches. Then, there was "Vulgar Latin." It was not called vulgar because it had lots of four-letter words or people used it to tell dirty jokes—it was spoken by the "vulgars," their word for the ordinary, everyday people.

Everyone spoke Vulgar Latin—even the "high class" folks, and little kids. But there were many versions of Vulgar Latin. So, in Spain, it sounded more like Spanish, and in France, it sounded awfully French, etc.* Sort of like our Southern accent (Y'all) versus a New England accent (You all).

So, Vulgar Latin eventually became several languages and the high class Latin was saved for books and speeches—(YAWN!) but not really spoken aloud any more.

The difference between high class and Vulgar Latin is sort of like this: We might write, or say to our teacher, "Do you understand?"… but we say to our friends, "Ya know?" Ya know what I mean? Gee, we'd better watch out, or good English might die out just like fancy Latin did!

P.S.**

*Etc. is Latin for *et cetera* or "and so on, and so forth."
**P.S. is Latin for *post script*, or "after the writing."

YOU KNOW LATIN ALREADY!

WHAT???!!!

Many of the words you use in your everyday conversation are either Latin or have Latin roots.

You know that a.m. is the time before lunch and p.m. is the time after lunch. Well, a.m. is just the abbreviation for the Latin words *ante meridiem* (before noon, when your stomach growls)—and p.m. is short for *post meridiem* (after noon, when you feel like a nice nap.)

If your parents went to college, their school was their *alma mater*, or "foster mother."

The *pro* and *con* reasons to go to school are just the reasons "for" or "against." (Surely you can think of one more reason pro than recess!)

If you like your teachers, and *vice versa*, then your teachers like you too. (Of course they do, silly!)

If school is over, you might go home *via* the school bus, *via* a car, or *via* moving your Nikes and your knees up and down. *Via*, obviously, means "by way of."

If it rains today and it rains tomorrow that is the *status quo*, or "the same old thing"—not to mention that the school picnic is now going to be held in the gym!

A *bona fide* friend is a genuine, true blue, let-you-borrow-anything friend.

A.D. is *anno domini* or in the year of our Lord. What is B.C.?—(besides a comic strip!)

On our great seal of the United States, there are three Latin phrases:

Annuit coeptis – "He has favored our undertakings."

Novus ordo seclorum – "A new world order"

E pluribus unum – "Out of many, one" (You heard that one, hey??!)

The U.S. Marine Corps and your dog share the same Latin motto—*Semper Fidelis*—which does not mean "Sit, Fido," it means "always faithful." Of course, the U.S. Coast Guard and your local Boy Scout are *semper paratus,* or "always prepared"—unless they forgot the peanut butter!

So see! Not only do you already know a lot of Latin, but you hear it and say it everyday.

And it doesn't hurt a bit, does it?

Now, go put your room in better *ordo* before your *alma mater* discovers the *status quo*—and you are in *bona fide* trouble!

(TRY SOME "LATIN" WRITING LIKE THIS ON YOUR OWN, USING THE WORDS YOU HAVE LEARNED SO FAR!]

_____

_____

_____

WHY LEARN LATIN?

Why bother to learn a language that is called—"DEAD?"

Well, it's true Latin isn't spoken by anyone anymore (except in some religious services.) But, LATIN LIVES!

The Roman Alphabet (you know A... B... C... !) is used today throughout most of the world.

Latin is also the basis of the "Romance languages" (*not* called this because boyfriends and girlfriends speak them!) The Romance languages are Italian, Spanish, French, Portuguese, and Romanian.

Even though English is not a Romance language, it has been greatly influenced by Latin, as you will see.

Roman numerals are also still used today: at the end of some people's names (Joe Blow, II); on the chapter headings of some books; as street numbers on some buildings; and on some clocks and watches.

Learning a little about Latin will also teach you new things about history, English, reading, writing—even that stuff called "grammar."

But, best of all, Latin is fun—even silly! Did you know that in Rome most people used chamber pots for bathrooms? They had a special place to empty them, but some lazy folks just dumped them out of their upstairs windows—onto the poor peoples' heads below!

YUCK!

HAPPY DAYS - ROMAN -STYLE

The family was very important to the Romans. The father was definitely the head of the household. He had complete power over his family and commanded obedience from his children. Fathers could even kill their sons! Even when this horrid practice was made illegal, they could still abandon their sons or leave them on a trash dump.

Boys went to school. Girls stayed home and learned to cook and sew and clean. (No wonder *they* didn't end up in the trash dump!) Boys would sneak off at recess to watch the chariot races. They had very long summer vacations, and at least **100** school holidays each year!

Schools weren't like our schools today. Classes were held in shops, on roof tops—anywhere a teacher could find room. Teachers could read and write, but that's about all—many of them had been fighters, racers, or even clowns!

When boys turned 17, they joined the army. They also had the *amulet* around their neck removed (which had been put there when they were only 9 days old to keep away the "evil eye"!) They also had their hair clipped for the first time. They dedicated this fuzzball to some Roman god and pinned it on a "hair tree" with their friends' hair.

Girls were engaged to be married when they were 10 years old. The father chose his daughter's husband while she was still a little girl. Some of the women who didn't want to marry fought as gladiators, rode in chariot races, or were wrestlers. Which would *you* choose?

"CRUISIN" – IN A CHARIOT

In ancient Rome, the government provided the entertainment and amusements for the people.

The *Campus Martius* was not a school. It was a large field set aside for athletic exercises and military training. Track and field events like running, jumping, archery and discus throwing were held here.

Dramatic plays, dance performances, and pantomimes were presented in open-air theatres.

Thermae or *balneae* were fancy baths with libraries, gyms, and gardens—sort of like swimming pools and country clubs, Roman-style!

Roman fights and races could really get rough. Criminals were often thrown out to wild animals and forced to fight. If they fell down and seemed to be dead, an attendant would rush out and hit them on the head with a hammer just to be sure! If they fought bravely, they were sometimes set free. How did the Emperor indicate his decision? With a "thumbs up"!

Many times, arenas were filled with water and pretend naval battles were staged.

EVERYONE, SHHHH!

Chariot races were the most popular; gladiator fights and wrestling matches were also favorites. Most of the big events were held in the *Circus Maximus,* a huge arena sort of like the Superdome. But, because it was wooden and caught fire easily, it collapsed many times, crushing thousands of people to death! Finally, it was rebuilt in stone and decorated with marble.

Chariot racing was so important to the Roman emperor that he sent troops out in the neighborhood to be sure no one made too much noise and disturbed his horse before a race. Caligula made his horse a Roman senator!

DRAW YOUR VERSION OF THE *CIRCUS MAXIMUS*.

TEMPUS FUGIT (TIME FLIES) LATIN TRIVIA

TO GO?—At Roman dinner parties guests often brought their own napkins to tie around their necks. When the dinner was finished, they would wrap up some leftover goodies in their napkins to take home!

O'CLOCK—If you had an appointment at a certain time, you might find yourself running late when it clouded up and you couldn't read your sundial!

WALK A MILE IN MY SHOES!—Romans wore sandals indoors and high shoes outdoors. The sandals we wear today were modeled after the Roman shoes.

QUEEN OF THE ROADS—Probably the most famous road in the world is the "Appian Way," which is still in use today—2,000 years after it was built!

HAPPY NEW YEAR!—The month of January was named after the Roman god, Janus—the god of beginnings.

TEMPUS FUGIT (TIME FLIES) MORE TRIVIA

POPEYE?—Olive oil was much valued by the Romans. It took the place of butter in cooking, was used for fuel in lamps for cleaning, in bathing, and making perfume and cosmetics. Can you write a "commercial" for Roman television for this useful product?

WHEN IN ROME…—"Do as the Romans do" goes a popular saying. So if you were a Roman woman, you would wear a lot of makeup, have an elaborate hairdo, and put as many rings on your fingers as you could!

A ROMAN MALL?—From dawn to dusk, wheeled traffic was forbidden in the city. People walked, rode mules, or were carried on litters by porters.

BRAVO!—A Roman lawyer sometimes hired an audience to come to court to applaud his speeches and perhaps sway the jury to his client's side.

EASY AS I CAME...

Read the following sentences. THEN REWRITE THE SENTENCES IN YOUR OWN WORDS. See if you can "translate" the Latin phrases into English. Make sure to do your work *summa cum laude*!

1. "She talks about her new boyfriend *ad nauseam*."

Answer: _____

2. "I wish summer vacation would go on *ad infinitum*."

Answer: _____

3. "I stuffed the *corpus delicti* under my bed!"

Answer: _____

4. "You can get your mouth washed out with soap for a *lapsus linguae*."

Answer: _____

5. "For homework, my *modus operandi* is to sprawl in front of the TV, with the stereo blasting and lots of junk food."

Answer: _____

6. "I ate 6 pizzas, 4 cheeseburgers, and 2 chocolate sundaes *in toto*."

Answer: _____   _____

7. "My mother cleaned my room when I was *in absentia*."

Answer: _____

8. "That new kid acts like he's *non compos mentis*."

Answer: _____

9. "Tell me *verbatim* what they said about me."

Answer: _____

10. "Clean up your *habitat*, and make your bed."

Answer: _____

Summa cum laude means with highest distinction.

NUMERO UNO

There are seven Roman numerals from which all Roman numbers can be written.

I =1   **V** =5   **X** =10   **L** =50

C =100   **D** =500   **M** =1,000

You write Roman numerals from left to right. The largest numeral is written first, then the smaller numerals after. You add them together to find out the number.

15 = XV (10+5)   115 = CXV (100+10+5)

116 = CXVI (100+10+5+1)

A special rule to remember is "don't repeat a letter more than three times." What do you do about a number like 4? You write a smaller numeral on the left of a larger numeral to subtract:

4 = IV (5 - 1)

74 = LXXIV (50+10+10+5-1)

How old are you? _____

(Ah, ah, ah ... in Roman numerals.) _____

Good! Now, what year were you born? In Roman numerals?

_____

NUMERO DUO

Now that you know Roman numerals, how about some math:

REMEMBER: *Numero No No*

(That's Latin for if this is not your book, then don't write in it!)

L - X = _____

D + C = _____

X + V + I = _____

V + V - I = _____

C + D = _____

M ÷ C = _____

X x X = _____

What number is: MMMCCCLXXXVI? Write your answer in the box!

(Don't ask me—my computer made it up!)

LATIN GRAFFITI

Ancient Romans loved to write stories, plays, and poems. They also wrote on walls! Some examples of Roman graffiti (written in Latin) still exist today. **Can you think of some graffiti to write? Here are some Latin words to help you.**

WRITE YOUR LATIN GRAFFITI HERE! *(If this is not your book, please use a separate piece of paper.)*

TE AMO - I love you
NOMEN - name
PUGNAS - fight
TEMPUS - time
ADE DOMUM - go home
DIESA - day
PAX - peace

NOX - night
AMICUS - friend
EGO - I
QUI? - Who?
ILLE - he
ILLA - she
ET - and

BONUS - good
DICO - I say
BREVIS - short
DO - I give
LABOR - work
PETO - I ask
PUTO - think

VOCE - call
SERVO - save
TU - you
QUIS? - What?
CUM - with

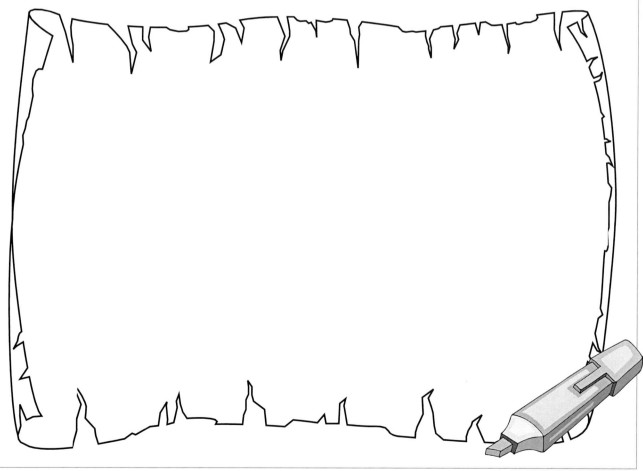

TEE SHIRT TOGA

The *toga* was a loose, draped cloth that Romans wore. Yes, it does look like they got out of bed and brought the sheet with them! Only citizens of Rome could wear the *toga*; it was the official formal dress, like tuxedos are for fancy affairs today.

Can you create a modern-day toga? You can add designs, color, and add a statement—like tee shirts of today! Use the word list to help you.

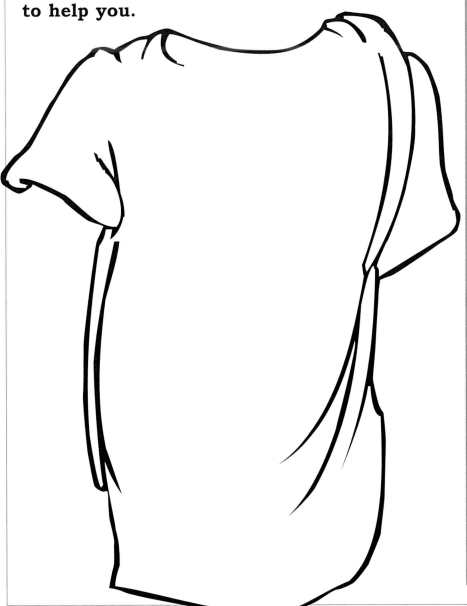

AESTAS - summer
IMPERATOR - general
AMICITIA - friendship
PAX - peace
ANIMUS - mind
REX - king
CASTRA - camp
FACILIS - easy
DUX - leader
LIBER - free
FEMINA - woman
MALUS - bad
FILIA - daughter
MEUS - my, mine
FILIUS - son
NOSTER - our, ours
FRATER - brother
ALTUS - high, deep
SPERO - I hope
TEMPTO - I try
VENIO - I come
VIDEO - I see
CIRCUM - around
CUR? - Why?
SED - but
VOLO - I wish
QUANTUS - how great
OMNIS - all, every
NOTUS - famous
EO - I go
HABEO - I have
PROPERO - I hurry
POSSUM - I can
SPECTO - I look at
SUM - I am
TRADO - I give
VOCO - I call
NUNC - now
ET - and

A LITTLE MORE LATIN

Latin nouns (like girl, boy, book) come in three different "genders"—masculine (like boy); feminine (like girl); and neutral (like body). This could get confusing. To Romans, water was feminine, so was an island. But land and books were masculine. Time and words were neutral nouns.

If you were a Roman baby boy, you could count on having three names: a *praenomen*, like your first name; a *nomen*, which was the name of your clan; and a *cognomen*, or a last name. If you did something really great in your life, you might get another name or *agnomen*.

If you were a Roman girl, you only got the feminine gender form of your father's *nomen*. So, all the girls had the same name in a family—and numbers (Suzy Q 1; Suzy Q 2) to tell them apart.

One of the most famous names in Roman history is that of Julius Caesar, one of the greatest generals of all times.

THERE IS A MONTH THAT WAS NAMED IN HONOR OF JULIUS CAESAR. UNSCRAMBLE THE LETTERS AND WRITE YOUR ANSWER BELOW.

_____

A LITTLE MORE LATIN

Even though the Romans were often cruel and involved in wars, they had some very special ideas which influenced people and civilizations long after them. For the Romans, whose Latin language had a very good word for everything, these important ideas were:

Pietas - a sense of duty

Gravitas - seriousness of purpose

Dignitas - a sense of personal worth

Many, many of our English words come from Latin, and even if you know just a little Latin, it will help you figure out the meaning of new English words you come across.

Here are a few examples of the connection between Latin and English words:

Liber means book; *libri* means books. Just like our *libr*aries!

Eques was the Latin word for horseman; we call them *eques*trians.

Praemium was a prize or reward; have you ever found a *premium* in your cereal box?

Porto meant I carry; today if something is *port*able, we can carry it from place to place.

CAN YOU THINK OF ANY OTHER LATIN WORDS YOU KNOW?

CAN YOU FIGURE OUT WHICH LATIN NUMBER GOES WITH WHICH ENGLISH NUMBER?

_____ **1.** How many years in a century?

_____ **2.** If you subtract five from this number, you will have five!

_____ **3.** How many sides does an octagon have?

_____ **4.** You are numero uno!

_____ **5.** What do you call two people singing together?

_____ **6.** How many years in a millennium?

_____ **7.** The car you ride in has this many wheels!

a. 1 (únus)   b. 2 (duo)   c. 8 (octó)

d. 100 (centum)   e. 1000 (mílle)   f. 10 (decem)

g. 4 (quattuor)

WHAT GRADE ARE YOU IN, LATIN-STYLE? (No hints, this time!)
PUT A CHECK NEXT TO YOUR ANSWER!

☐ Primus?   ☐ Quartus?   ☐ Septimus?

☐ Secundus?   ☐ Quintus?   ☐ Octavus?

☐ Tertius?   ☐ Sextus?   ☐ Nonus?

USE THE CLUES!

CAN YOU FIGURE OUT THE MEANING OF THESE LATIN WORDS?
WRITE THE ENGLISH WORD FOR THE LATIN WORD IN ITALICS?

1. At the carnival, I let the lady with the crystal ball tell my *fortuna*.

_____

2. There was really a *multitudo* of people and cars at the rock concert.

_____

3. If I *invenio* my lost homework before class, I'll be so happy. Rhymes with (not brain!) ☛

_____

4. May the *vis* be with you!

_____

5. The next time they send a rocket to the *luna*, I want to be on it!

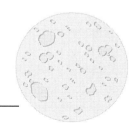

_____

CHOICES! CHOICES!

ANSWER THESE MULTIPLE CHOICE QUESTIONS:

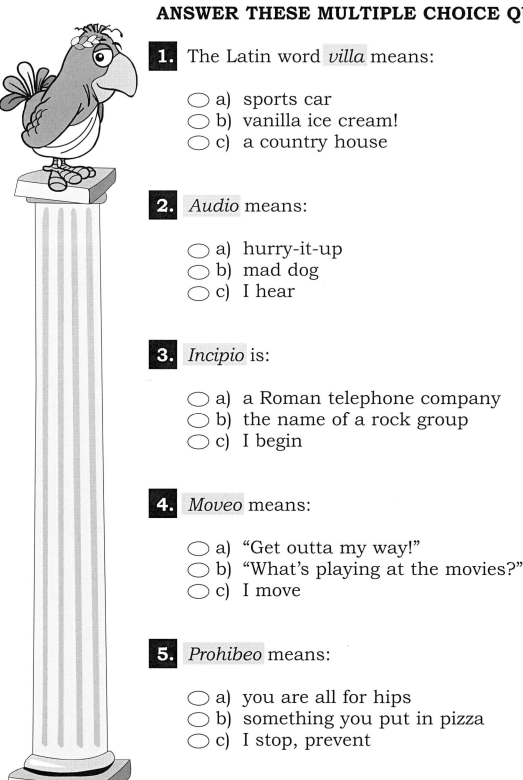

1. The Latin word *villa* means:

  ○ a) sports car
  ○ b) vanilla ice cream!
  ○ c) a country house

2. *Audio* means:

  ○ a) hurry-it-up
  ○ b) mad dog
  ○ c) I hear

3. *Incipio* is:

  ○ a) a Roman telephone company
  ○ b) the name of a rock group
  ○ c) I begin

4. *Moveo* means:

  ○ a) "Get outta my way!"
  ○ b) "What's playing at the movies?"
  ○ c) I move

5. *Prohibeo* means:

  ○ a) you are all for hips
  ○ b) something you put in pizza
  ○ c) I stop, prevent

LEARN LATIN

USE THE WORD BANK TO LEARN THE MEANING OF THESE LATIN WORDS.

WORD BANK

1. When *absum* from school, I'm not there!

_____

2. When you live *trans* the road you live _____ the road.

_____

3. *Meritto* my friend to borrow my best sweater.

_____

4. Are you *iam* tired of school and ready for summer vacation?

_____

5. When *respondeo* to my parents' questions I am always polite.

_____

6. When you *circum* the block you go _____ it.

_____

7. When *rogo* my mother to stay out later, she says, "yes."

_____

I ask

across

already

absent

I answer

I allow

around

8. *Quod* you've cleaned up your room (and did a good job), you can go out with your friends.

_____

9. If you're *inter* a rock and a hard place, you are:

_____

10. When *fero* home a good report card my parents are thrilled.

_____

11. How many *liberi* are in your school?

_____

12. Do you live in the country or in the *urbs*?

_____

13. Can you *venio* and go as you please? (Best not!)

_____

14. I much prefer the *rus* life over the city, don't you?

_____

WORD BANK

children

between

country

I bring, carry

city

because

come

Stay focused on the finish!

15. How *facio* you *facio*?

_____

16. *Ago* to school now that I have a permit.

_____

17. Some things are difficult, some things impossible, but Latin is *facilis*! Don't you think so?

_____

18. When will this quiz *finis*?

_____

19. It's not right to *pugna*. Don't you agree?

_____

20. We should always try to put our best *pes* forward!

_____

21. If you ask your parents if you can have a *comparo* this Saturday and the answer is yes, can I come?

_____

Keep up the good work!

22. I think taking this quiz is a *magnus* idea!

_____

23. Let me give you a *manus*. (Clue: You have two of these!)

_____

24. You have a good *caput* on your shoulders!

_____

25. *Teneo* my room clean most of the time!

_____

26. The wind was blowing my hat so hard *dimitto* of it.

_____

27. Please turn the *lux* on.

_____

28. "Twinkle, twinkle, *parvus* star, how I wonder what you are."

_____

I let go

head

great

little

hand

I keep

light

You're almost there!

29. This is the *longus* and short of it.

_____

30. Are you a *vir* or a mouse? You don't have to answer that if you don't want to!

_____

31. Sometimes we have more *pecunia* than others. (It's been said that it's also the root of all evil!)

_____

32. When I am lonesome *appello* my friends on the telephone.

_____

33. *Pono* my fax number on the bulletin board.

_____

34. *Mitto* invitations to my birthday party over the Internet.

_____

35. Do you and your *soror* get along well?

_____

WORD BANK

I call

long

I send

sister

man

money

I put

Just a little bit more!

36. *Intermitto* for stop signs!

_____

37. Who is referred to as the *fortis* man of the world? HERCULES!

_____

38. *Capio* the school bus on rainy mornings.

_____

39. I sure do enjoy summer much more than *hiems*. Don't you?

_____

40. *Sine* your allowance, you'd be in a fine fix! Don't you agree?

_____

41. HI-HO, HI-HO! It's off to *laboro* we go.

_____

42. *Tu* are smart to figure out the answers to these questions!

_____

Excellent! I knew *you* could do it!

ANSWER KEY

Page 14–15: 1. 'Til it makes us sick!; 2. To infinity or, at least 'til Christmas!; 3. The body, as in dead; 4. Slip of the tongue; 5. Method of working; 6. The whole thing!; 7. Gone — just like all the good stuff you had stashed under the bed!; 8. Crazy!; 9. Word for word; 10. Room (literally one's surroundings)

Page 16. Answers will vary.

Page 17: 1. 40; 2. 600; 3. 16; 4. 9; 5. 600; 6. 10; 7. 100 (NUMBER IN THE BOX = 3,386

Page 20: July

Page 22: 1. D; 2. F; 3. C; 4. A; 5. B; 6. E; 7. G

Page 23: 1. Fortune; 2. Multitude/Many; 3. Find; 4. Force; 5. Moon

Page 24: 1. C; 2. C; 3. C; 4. C; 5. C

Page 25: 1. Absent; 2. Across; 3. I allow; 4. Already; 5. I answer; 6. Around; 7. I ask

Page 26: 8. Because; 9. Between; 10. I bring, carry; 11. Children; 12. City; 13. Come; 14. Country

Page 27: 15. Do; 16. I drive; 17. Easy; 18. End; 19. Fight; 20. Foot; 21. Get together

Page 28: 22. Great; 23. Hand; 24. Head; 25. I keep; 26. I let go; 27. Light; 28. Little

Page 29: 29. Long; 30. Man; 31. Money; 32. I call; 33. I put; 34. I send; 35. Sister

Page 30: 36. I stop; 37. Strong; 38. I take; 39. Winter; 40. Without; 41. Work; 42. You

I am so very proud of you. You did an awesome job!

CERTIFICATE OF ACHIEVEMENT

This Certificate of Achievement is to bear witness that

Name: _____

officially completed this book and can speak Latin.

Signed: _____ *Dr. G.E. Nius* _____   Date: _____